A Kingdom Waiting:
Loss, Triumph and the Young Spirit

Edited by

Sarah Acton

Published by

Passionate Pens
An imprint of Pen of the Writer, LLC
Dayton, Ohio
PassionatePens.com

Published by
Passionate Pens an
imprint of
Pen of the Writer, LLC
Dayton, Ohio
PenOfTheWriter.com

Copyright © 2011 by Trotwood-Madison Senior High School

All rights reserved. No part of this book may be reproduced or transmitted in any form or by any means, electronic or mechanical, without prior written consent of the Publisher, except for the inclusion of brief quotes in a review.

Passionate Pens—an imprint of Pen of the Writer—is committed to promoting youth literacy.

Library of Congress Control Number: 2011905217

ISBN-13: 978-0-9825984-5-0

Cover design by Charlotte L. Brown
Edited by Sarah Acton, Creative Writing Teacher and
Valerie J. Lewis Coleman of PenOfTheWriter.com

Printed in the United States of America

Table of Contents

Acknowledgements 8
A Kingdom Waiting 9
   By Sarah Acton

You and Me 12
   By Renika Williams

My City 14
   By Renon Lorenzo

The Loss of a Sister 15
   By Lydia Hanns

A Loss of Emotion 17
   By Maria Rabb

I Don't Remember 19
   By Taylor Davenport

A Loss of Madness 21
   By Bobby R. Smith Jr.

An Unsent Letter 23
   By Korey Beavers

Losing Myself 25
   By Bryanna Jackson

A Loss of Loved Ones 26
   By Davonn Stollings

Living by Faith 28
   By Courtney McFadden

The Kindness She Carried 30
   By Jasmine Thompson

This is a Goodbye 32
   By Asha Wooten

A Dangerous Thought 35
    By Tiera Robinson

Dedicated to My Grandfather 38
    By Michael Geter

My Loss 39
    By Latasia Holt

Now He's Gone 40
    By Shatora George

My Fear 42
    By Tionna Towler

Grandpa Was a Rolling Stone 44
    By Aleshia Burt

Loss of My Former Self 46
    By Darnell Edwards

Letting Go 48
    By Chaelyn Allen

To All My Wonderful Grandmas in Heaven 49
    By Ciera Avery

Never Judge a Book by Its Cover 51
    By Jamae Finch

You Never Know What You Have 55
    By Precious Carmichael

Emotionally Missing 56
    By Brandon Davenport

Trust 58
    By Kenny Cochran

A Letter to Myself 60
    By Elisha Street

My G-Mom 62
    By Alexis Davis

Loss of a Father, Growth of a Child 66
   By Desiaire Rickman

Losing Myself in Shadows 69
   By Ebony Munday

The Loss of Trust 71
   By Chrisha Taylor

I Will Never Forget 72
   By Shaunice Passmore

A Loss of Memory 73
   By Michael Booze

The Strongest Man I Knew 74
   By Krysta Coleman

Swimming 76
   By Auston Smith

My Biggest Reality Check 77
   By Jasmine Owensby

All For the Best 78
   By Kendra Crowe

That Will Never Be Me 80
   By Tonisha Williamson

The Burden of Betrayal 81
   By Brytni Morris

Best Friends, Like Sisters 82
   By Brandee Femuels

Lesson Learned 84
   By Asia Buycks

About the Contributors 87
Passionate Pens 93

Acknowledgements

Gerald Cox—Human Resources Director of Trotwood City Schools—connected with the publisher at a community networking event. He said, "I want you to do something with Trotwood students," and then put the wheels in motion.

Terry Logan—Principal of Trotwood-Madison High School—believed in the students and sponsored the project.

Valerie J. Lewis Coleman—creator of the Passionate Pens—co-edited and published the anthology.

Sarah Acton—Creative Writing Teacher—typed, compiled and co-edited the anthology.

And the wonderful students who let their hearts spill onto the pages of this book.

A Kingdom Waiting

By Sarah Acton

There is nothing like youth. The middle-aged are mortgaged to life. The old are in life's lumber room. But youth is the lord of life. Youth has a kingdom waiting for it. Everyone is born a king, and most people die in exile, like most kings.
~ Oscar Wilde

Oscar Wilde was obsessed with the idea of youth, both in his life and his work. Dorian Gray, his most famous character, was equally obsessed with youth and the beauty that accompanies it. But to see this fascination as a shallow, purely physical pursuit is to misconstrue Wilde's point about the true nature of youth. When he writes that "youth has a kingdom waiting for it," he means that the young have potential and possibility that those who are past youth no longer have. The world is limitless to the young. The more we age, the more limited our possibilities.

If you read Shakespeare, you will notice the same pattern. Who are the most interesting characters? In *Hamlet*, who intrigues us more, the king who murdered his own brother then married his brother's wife to usurp the throne or the prince who should have inherited the throne? Hamlet is the most intriguing character in part because he still had everything in front of him: college, marriage and the monarchy. This fact is also true in *Macbeth*. When Macbeth is vying for the throne, ruthlessly killing and scheming, he is far more interesting than when he has it. Once he is king, the play loses some of its appeal. We are innately drawn to the characters that are pursuing potential rather than the ones living it.

Consider the movies you love. Which characters are most worthwhile to watch on screen? Did you find that the first *Matrix* movie was better than the two sequels? Neo was more interesting as he strived to become "the one" than once he fulfilled his ambitions and potential. The last of the trilogy was especially hard to watch. Whether attributed to a convoluted plot or weak special effects, it lacked the suspense, intrigue and thrill of average Thomas A. Anderson morphing into extraordinary Neo.

Our culture's obsession with youth is partly a shallow fixation with beauty and perfection, but it's not entirely superficial and unwarranted. If we balanced the respect of wisdom—derived from age and experience—with the excitement and possibilities of youth, how different would life be?

Remember when youth meant not knowing realities and limits? I wanted to be president. I had no idea what that entailed, but the possibility existed. Isn't that exciting? As I grew older, I considered careers in medicine, art, journalism and theater. Now—not quite middle aged—I have made most of my decisions: college, career, husband, where I live, the number of children I have. So, when I considered writing a piece on loss, I thought about a type of loss that often goes undetected until it's long gone: loss of possibilities.

I'm of the glass-half-empty philosophy. I see the world as Wilde did. He knew that for as much as we gain through living, we lose through aging. And though we do not regularly articulate it, then loss is something we will inevitably experience on some level. We watch shows like *Toddlers and Tiaras* and wonder what drives parents to behave like that. Could it be that the inability to cope with the lost possibilities of youth causes parents to live vicariously through their children? By the time we have children, almost all potential energy has shifted to reality, a kind of static energy. Admit it: potential is more thrilling.

This observation may account for the high divorce rate as well. Potentially marrying someone is enchanting and exciting, but the realities of marriage can be mundane. It's difficult to prepare for the work needed to make marriage successful because our vision is blurred with intoxicating possibilities.

I'm simplifying. Of course not all pageant mothers attempt to live through their children and not all marriages end in divorce for the same reason; however, how much better would we be, if we had effective ways to cope with the missed possibilities of youth? Some take solace in the belief that God set this path and rarely look back at what could have been. Others find a way to retain the excitement and possibilities of youth.

One way I deal with this inevitable loss is through teaching. Helping young men and women find their way and make choices that will lead them to live out their potential takes me back to the exhilaration of youth. Admittedly, I experience a vicarious thrill watching the endless possibilities stretch into their futures.

When you read their stories, you will experience the unbounded possibilities of these amazing individuals with incredible talent. In addition to the enjoyment of reading about their struggles and triumphs, I dare say that you will be astounded at their maturity and aplomb, and blessed by their ability to share experiences. I thank them for all they have given me. Each of them truly has a kingdom waiting.

You and Me

By Renika Williams

The day I realized I had lost you, I wondered why it took me so long to see that you were missing. Crying out for you. Begging for you to come back. I beat myself up every day because I shouldn't have let you go in the first place. Who are you? You are me.

Me. Passionate and understanding. Sensitive...yet, dramatic. Caring and friendly. I've always had the desire to have a voice. I've always wanted to be strong and invincible. So, I created you and lost me.

You. Blunt and assertive. Daring and fearless. Heartless and cold. Centered and driven. You were everything I wanted to be.

As I entered high school, I felt I'd only survive if I portrayed myself as you. I wanted so badly to be you that I lost the things about me that were special. The beauty of me is that she's unique. One of a kind. So, why couldn't she be both me and you? Why couldn't I be a confident, emotional, bold, drama-queen all in one girl? The sad thing about it is that I could be all in one. I just didn't know it at the time.

You turned out to be a cold-hearted person who didn't care about the remarks made to others with piercing looks that cut deeply. But, even then I hadn't completely lost me. I was only you at school. Until...you started to come home with me.

I put up a brick wall around my heart because I was afraid it would shatter like so many times before. By age sixteen, I had already been lied to, cheated on, deceived and taken advantage of in past relationships. Hurt.

I back-talked my parents and argued with my brother. My family saw the change in me, but by then you were uncontrollable. Who was this mean-spirited person my loved ones couldn't stand, but attracted everyone else? Not me. I lost me. I lost the girl who was there when I got home, sitting crossed-legged on the sofa, reading for hours. I lost the girl who had a grin from ear to ear; sunrise to sunset; 365 days a year.

I let so many people influence my ways at school that eventually, that's who I had become. Now, I fight the battle between you and me. I am truly happy when I am myself. I am sorry I ever let her go. When I lost me, I learned so many lessons and suffered so many consequences because I was trying to be you. But, I will not mourn it...because the real me will grow from it.

Who are you? You are me.

My City

By Renon Lorenzo

I remember the exact moment I lost trust in my city—Dayton, Ohio. It was one of the most shocking and surprising days of my life.

The day started like any other. My brother and I were at his friend's house playing games, having fun. As usual, we ordered pizza, but the delivery guy was late. About thirty minutes later, we heard a knock on the door. My brother opened the door, but no one was there. A couple minutes later, we heard another knock. My brother answered again, but this time to a pistol in his face.

I ran to the kitchen and grabbed a long knife. The man held up my brother for about three minutes, asking if he had drugs or money. Well, he didn't ask as much as demand. He told us to give him the money or he would shoot.

I know that the Lord was there. The pizza delivery man pulled up. He pushed the door into the attacker which caught him off guard. With him distracted, I ran from the kitchen and sliced into the thug's hand—the one holding the gun. He dropped his pistol and my brother kicked it away.

Without his gun, he was no match for us. We beat him, until he finally got to his feet and ran out of the house. He didn't get far. The delivery man had called the police and they caught him in no time.

Although the man who threatened us was caught, on that day, I lost trust in my city: the City of Dayton.

The Loss of a Sister

By Lydia Hanns

Someone once told me that when you lose someone close to you, you don't mourn for them, you mourn for yourself.

My big sister, Shanté, was my best friend. She was so unique and always knew how to make me happy. Shanté had cerebral palsy, so she couldn't walk or talk and she was fed through a G-tube in her stomach.

I was an outcast. I've always been ridiculed by others and I often came home from school miserable. But as soon as I saw my sister, I felt better. If she could lie in bed in pain all day with a smile on her face, then why was it so hard for me? I told myself to suck it up and then I told Shanté about my day. She listened and laughed. I felt better.

On January 2, 2007, at seventeen years old, Shanté died from pneumonia. Four years later, it hurts more than ever because I'm seventeen. I think about how she was at this age. I could never be as good as Shanté. She was always an angel. No one compares. I realized that it was easy for me to express my feelings to her because she never criticized me. She just listened.

I used to think that the Lord took her away from me because I depended on her too much. I thought God was angry with me and I felt responsible for Him taking her away. Life seems so much harder without her, without someone to talk to. Pessimism set in and blocked out everyone. The pain was ineffable. Losing someone close to you is like losing a part of yourself.

Illuminations said, "An unrevealed part of yourself is never understood."

I've learned that it is important to not hold it in when you lose someone close to you. Building a wall and keeping to yourself will only add more pain and suffering. Find a way to let it out and deal with the loss; talk about your feelings, write a letter.

The way you cope, no matter how well it seems to work, is simply a mask for the pain.
~ Illuminations

A Loss of Emotion

By Maria Rabb

Lately, I haven't been able to reason. Emptiness surrounds me. I can't make up my mind on simple things. I haven't been able to think or feel anything.

Where have my emotions gone? It was even hard for me to write this story because my mind was blank. I can't cry anymore. A wetness forms in my eyes, but nothing comes out. My tears just dry up the moment they are made.

I hate this. I like to cry, to vent. But lately, nothing. Emotionless. Sometimes, I think it's because when a person has been through so much pain, she gets used to it. It doesn't hit as hard. It can't be that, though. I'm sure that millions of people have been through situations much worse than mine and they can cry about it, even years after. So, why can't I?

Maybe being a mother shocked me. It was so sudden; I never thought it would happen to me. Maybe motherhood made me strong and some sort of shock absorber blocked or erased my feelings.

Even when I want to be sad, I smile. When I'm depressed or stressed, I laugh. Despite all my emptiness, I laugh more. I think I laugh to hide my pain and true feelings. I love to laugh, but not when I really want to break down and cry.

Maybe I don't want to come off as a weak person, so I play it off. Then again, when have I ever cared about what others thought of me? I don't know where my feelings have gone. I wish my emotions would return. I don't know what I'm doing without them.

I want to cry and be upset about normal things. I want to hate certain things and get annoyed, but lately, all that is gone. Even though they're gone, I still care about things. I still love things. I still smile through the bad. So, what's wrong with me? I shouldn't have to force a reaction. I'm scared that one day, all my problems and all the things that cause me pain, will catch up with me. I'm going to lose control: cry until my eyes can't make tears, say bad things, become violent.

These built-up feelings that my body won't let me release will come to a boil. Maybe it will happen at the wrong moment, in front of the wrong person, in front of my daughter.

Maybe not being able to express my emotions is a good thing. Maybe I need to forgive and forget. Maybe I should live my life and be happy, smiling all the while. Maybe my loss of emotions is good.

I Don't Remember

By Taylor Davenport

I don't remember you ever being there. I almost don't remember you at all.

I don't remember you being at the hospital during labor. Mommy has pictures of me after I was born, but you weren't in a single one. I know you always said that you cared about me, but how am I supposed to know?

I don't remember you being at the church when I was baptized. Mom has pictures of that event, too. I didn't see you.

I can say, in fact, that you were never there for an important event in my life. You were not at birthday parties. You didn't show up on Christmas, Thanksgiving or Easter. You didn't go to any soccer games (I bet you didn't even know that I used to play soccer, did you?) Or dance recitals. (Yes, I used to dance ballet, too.) Or school plays.

You suck as a father.

You didn't bother to pick me up on your assigned weekends. You didn't call to check on me. You only picked me up when you wanted to show off "your little girl." (I was never your little girl. I hated when you called me that.)

When people ask me about my parents, I say, "I don't have a dad." It's true. I never count you as my dad. You were...no, you are a figment of my imagination. So faint. So distant. So unimportant. So dead to me.

I remember the day you called my house and asked to talk to me. I didn't want to speak to you. You were lucky I picked up the phone at all. I don't remember the exact conversation, but I do remember saying that I don't want to have anything to do with you.

Before that call, I hadn't heard from you in years. After that call, I didn't hear from you at all.

That was it.

The father-daughter relationship was over.

I hung up, let out a sigh of relief and then laughed. I found it hilarious that you thought you could come back into my life after five years of absence.

You're absent for good now.

I'm perfectly content without you.

Because of the predicament you're in, you won't see me graduate from high school or college.

I'm glad you aren't a part of my life. I'm doing much better without you. I don't remember why I ever thought I needed you in the first place.

A Loss of Madness

By Bobby R. Smith Jr.

When my dad passed away, I thought I couldn't make it. I don't know what was wrong with me. I was quick to give up, catch an attitude and stay mad all day.

I just wanted to say, "Thank you, Mrs. Acton." You teach differently than most teachers. Regardless of what other students may say or think, you helped me to keep my head up. I hope you understand how much you helped me change my life around.

Although I still think about how people acted after my dad's death, I learned to forgive them. It was hard, but I forgave them because I felt that my daddy would have wanted me to. I learned that madness was a feeling that only produced more hurt and pain. Thanks to you, I no longer feel that way.

My daddy always wanted me to be successful and I'm trying my best to make that happen. Also, I wanted you to know that the people who did such terrible things to me—and my dad's memory—will be held accountable in Court. I'm not going to lie. I've been scared and worried. I haven't told anyone how scared I really was. I've learned through your help and others who care about me that I can stand, not just as a man, but as one who can withstand anything.

I lost more than madness. I lost the bad feelings that caused me to make mistakes. God sent an angel to help me overcome my struggles and that angel was you. I couldn't show you all my happiness because I haven't felt good in a long time.

I want you to know that I will no longer let others get to me. I don't want to feel that pain anymore! I miss my daddy and I know he's looking down on me, smiling. I just have to make sure I keep doing the right things.

    I am going to keep thanking you because you showed me a way to get through. I appreciate the things you did for me. You gave me the strength to walk away from madness.

An Unsent Letter

By Korey Beavers

Dear Grandpa,

It's been three years since you passed. I ask myself if the legacy you left me is worth it. As a young Christian man, it seems like I can't have fun. I remember your smile, how brave you were and the fact that your knowledge of the Bible was untouchable.

People at church say that I'm going to be the next pastor. I wonder if I will ever have the knowledge that you had. At the age of eighty-one, you still worked. I pray that you will come down from Heaven and give me wisdom. You never come.

People ask me if I've ever been through anything. I close my eyes, smile and say, "No." But on the inside, I want to tell them what I have been through. I want to let them know what I have deep down on the inside.

I'm out of my mind without you. My soul—which was once filled with color—has transformed into black and white. My heart is concrete and the hand that holds it has been weathered by storm. The hand drops and there goes my heart. Shattered into a million pieces, throwing my anger around, breaking the glass to my soul. The devil's demons are working to take my soul to hell. Since you're gone, I tune out everyone. I want to be alone, so I can get along with my demons.

I try to cover the pain, but when the pain becomes unbearable, I break down and cry. Maybe I should cry or maybe I shouldn't.

All I know is that I miss you, and I want you back. I love you so much. I'm going to carry on your legacy because that is what you would want me to do.

Your grandson,

Korey

Losing Myself

By Bryanna Jackson

Can I be considered selfish because I want so much from so many people? I need attention. I want everyone to be here for me and only me. I guess I'm selfish because I never felt like I got the attention from my parents that my sisters and brothers have. I was left out of the fun and excitement throughout the house, so I looked for attention elsewhere.

Once I found that one person who cared for me, I never wanted him to go. I did almost anything to keep him with me. Although I limited my actions, I never limited my feelings for him.

One day, I must have given the wrong impression because the person I thought cared for me wanted that one thing. No matter what I said or did, he took it. I lost all respect for myself that day. I didn't confide in anyone. I placed myself in a little bubble.

Everything started to fall apart. I lost everything. I felt as if no one ever wanted to just be there for me. So, I gave up.

My life was nothing to me. Not even God could help me. Well, that's what I thought. After months of being by myself and losing everything, I decided that someone should know.

It took a while for me to stop crying every night. I didn't need attention—all I needed was to get more involved. I stayed mad at myself because I didn't learn that earlier. Maybe my situation would be different if I had.

I've changed a lot over the years. I have a few people who support me and I'm doing much better. I know that I don't need anyone, but myself to keep me going.

A Loss of Loved Ones

By Davonn Stollings

I've lost many loved ones. Some took me a while to get over, but some were more easily forgotten. I know that sounds harsh, but that's what is best for me.

My losses started when I lost someone who took great care of me: my grandpa. When he got sick, I was in the fourth grade. When he was in the hospital, he told me and my brothers to never let anyone or anything tear apart our family. He died of old age in a nursing home.

When I was in the fifth grade, my uncle died in a motorcycle accident. He wasn't wearing a helmet when he ran into a truck that was reversing. He went head first off the bike and died instantly. Though I didn't know him well, he was a caring and helpful uncle.

My seventh and eighth-grade years were the worst because I lost seven people to whom I was close. One cousin died from an enlarged heart. I remember playing basketball with my cousin, but now he's gone. Five friends were killed by guns and hit-and-runs. My uncle was shot and killed at a park. They all had a part in my life, and I will never forget them.

Going into my freshmen year of high school, I thought all the chaos would be over, but at the end of the year, my best friend died three days after my birthday. When she tried to stop her boyfriend from arguing with someone, he pulled out a gun and accidentally shot her. The bullet entered through one side and came out of the other. Not only was that the first time I had seen someone get shot, it was the first time I saw someone bleed like that.

Because of the loved ones I've lost during my lifetime, I tell people to love and cherish family and friends. No matter how much you may fight, argue or dislike each other, you have to love them. My loss has taught me to appreciate what I have and I'm glad for the people in my life.

Living by Faith

By Courtney McFadden

Just before my eighteenth birthday, I remember I was happy. Happy about life, until it was stolen from me. Stolen, gone, a piece of me, my dreams, my self-worth. A relationship buried in the cold ground covered with pain and regret. A doctor's visit that changed my life forever.

I used to think that I was invincible until reality knocked me down. I still stumble, trying to get back up. I was in a relationship with the enemy—a liar who had a secret. This secret stayed sealed behind his lips.

In pain, I walked into the cold waiting room, no one there to comfort me. I dragged myself back to the doctor's room and sat. *Accept the worst, but hope for the best*, I repeated in my head. And it was just that: the worst. I figured that I didn't pray hard enough. The doctor scheduled a follow-up appointment.

I grew up too fast because I have to deal with this for the rest of my life. I felt worthless. One of my goals after college was to get married and have children. After the doctor uttered the diagnosis, I felt that I would never love again or get married. How will I find a dream guy to accept me and my dysfunction?

My emotions went through many changes. Jokes or activities that used to make me happy became my personal hell. I was depressed. So, when my eighteenth birthday came two days later, it was bittersweet. I tried to be happy, but found myself balled up in a corner, holding my knees tight to my chest. Tears flowed uncontrollably, until I gave myself headaches. I cried myself to sleep and woke up only to look in the mirror with disgust and cry some more.

I couldn't fathom how he could know about this filthy indiscretion and not tell me. Why did I have to find out the hard way? At the very least, he owed me an apology. When I asked for one, he said, "You'll get over it." I hung up the phone and we never talked again.

I began each day with a cry and then a prayer.

He spread rumors about me. My heart sank. Until, I got tired of wallowing in my misery.

I prayed more. My relationship with God became closer than ever. We bonded daily. He was my new best friend. My grandmother spoke to me about living by faith and not by sight. And it was so—I lived by faith. I felt increments of relief each day. Waking up wasn't as hard. God had been working day-by-day to relieve me of the burdens I carried. He worked to rebuild my self-worth and helped me to love myself again.

I read about and met people who dealt with the same situation. I had hope again. People like me do get married and have children. My philosophy: it could be worse and I'm not going to die from it, so why not live life to the fullest?

As for him, he stays in my prayers. My grandmother taught me that I shouldn't be vengeful. God loves everyone, so I let go. I look at this experience as a closed chapter in the book of my life. And as one chapter ends, another opens. I have dreams to catch!

The Kindness She Carried

By Jasmine Thompson

On July 19, 2010, I lost my friend, Amanda. She had heart surgery. She made it through the surgery, but after two days, her heart failed. The doctors took her off some machine before her heart was ready. Her death made me realize how short life can be. She didn't even get to see her sixteenth birthday.

I met Amanda in the summer of 2009 at the University of Dayton's Upward Bound program. The first day we met, I knew she was a sweet girl with a gentle and loving personality. She had the prettiest gold, curly hair. A doll! Even though there were times when I would be mean to her, she never stopped being my friend. The kindness she carried was what made me love her.

After the summer program, I didn't see her as much. At the Upward Bound events held through the year, I wondered where she was. Little did I know, she was having trouble with her heart again.

In the summer of 2010, she returned and told us that she wouldn't be able to stay the whole summer. She explained how she had her first heart surgery when she was only three days old. Then, she was too young to be scared, but now, at age fifteen, she knew the possible outcomes of the surgery.

She left about three weeks into the summer. Her heart was overworked because she was so restless. She told us that she was scared of dying, but hoped she would be okay. I never even thought that she wouldn't make it through her surgery.

I remember the night Jazmaine called and told me that Amanda was gone. I was stunned. I went to her Facebook page and read comments saying that she would be missed and they couldn't believe she was gone. I cried. I stared at her profile picture. I couldn't believe that the pretty girl who was so nice was gone.

The day of her funeral was tough for me. Seeing her lie there, so cold, so still, terrified me. I looked at her and shook my head. Her mom stared at her, unable to cry, just dazed. I know that her heart broke having to bury her daughter.

They threw Amanda a birthday party and played all of the music she enjoyed. I couldn't celebrate knowing she was gone.

Seven months after she left us, I still couldn't grasp the idea that Amanda was gone. It's crazy how life goes on, even after your loved ones leave this earth.

I love you, Amanda. And I want you to know that I always think of you. I still hear you whisper, "Hi, Jasmine."

R.I.P. Amanda Washington
August 1, 1994 – July 19, 2010

This is a Goodbye

By Asha Wooten

Dear Jabari,

It's funny how I no longer feel the need to call you Dad. I'm eighteen and have neither one of my parents. I like to think that you both were too young to take care of me.

I don't have a lot of memories. All I have is a random mix of moments—let downs, mostly. I wish you had never entered my life because the random in-and-outs hurt twice as much as not knowing you at all. I learned this year that my mom wanted to leave the city when I was young. I wish she would have because that would explain the distance I feel. To live a ten-minute walk away and still have you ignore me; painful.

I was only worth your time when it came to money; a paycheck. You didn't even want me in your wedding. The few times you came around, you and my mother were hell-bent on who paid what and when.

I remember every moment. Like the time I was at Kettering Youth Services. I tried to run to your house, but ended up crying and rocking in the mud because you didn't want to be bothered with me.

For the first time in years, you bought me a Christmas gift. I cried. I even left my boyfriend's house after only being there for five minutes because Aunt Lisha and Kiki urged me to come to see you. When I hugged you, you looked puzzled and didn't hug back. But that's okay. I was happy.

You didn't want to dance with me at my cotillion, and I thought it wouldn't bother me. It did. Yet again, I wished I never knew you. You used to care about me; you used to think twice about me. I used to get "I miss you" and birthday cards. You used to love me. "Used to" was a long time ago.

I love every moment with you, even if it's a bitter reminder of what little time we spend together. I still have my *Disney Princess Story* book. I wore those pink and white Jordans until the pink faded and the white was a horrible beige. The flower anklet you bought me meant so much that I wanted to show it off to everyone. I wore it on my wrist as a bracelet for weeks after Christmas.

You hit me. Like a child riding a bike and smacking the hard concrete, you caught me off guard. If only I had gotten in the shower when you told me. I remember when you chased me from the house as you headed toward me with a knife. Your wife watched; she did nothing to stop you or help me. I'm not her or my mother. They took your beatings. I guess I am more like you—I throw punches, push, fight and talk down. Without thinking twice, you told everyone that I attacked you.

You never wanted me. I didn't have light skin or curly hair. I was the opposite. I'm eighteen, grown and you haven't been there to do anything.

I wish I could come to you when I need advice from a male authority figure. I don't know how to carry myself or interact with men and because of you I don't want kids or a family. It's too dirty, too grimy. You taught me that men can't be trusted and women are of no value. You shaped me into who I am and how I act. I hate my last name. Instead of Asha Wooten, I want people to call me Asha Joilene.

I wanted to be like you. I said my favorite football team was the Raiders. I told people that my middle name was Hasni because that was yours. I wanted so badly to have you here with me. I dreamed, hoped, wished one day you would be here. But you never were. You were a dream.

I want to forgive you. I want you to see how amazing I am. I don't want you to say that you're sorry. I just want a reason—a reason why I wasn't worth the investment of time. But, I'm letting go now.

This is a goodbye.

Asha Joilene

A Dangerous Thought

By Tiera Robinson

I used to watch other people just to observe them and their actions. Often as I looked around, trying to imagine what they were thinking, I saw other young females, and my wandering imagination kicked into overload. Silly thoughts popped in my head, one after another, like fireworks.

Does she think she's better than me? Does she think she's prettier than me? Does she have any of the same flaws that I have? Is she making fun of me in her head?

Then, I'd think, *No, never mind. Why would someone even be thinking about me?*

Again, the thoughts started. *Does she have a lot of self-confidence? Confidence I don't have. I bet she probably gets lots of attention. What's wrong with me?*

I tried to answer these questions, which made me feel worse. Selfishness polluted my brain, causing me to relate every thought back to myself. Insecurity was the toxin in my mind that made me cry when I looked at my reflection in the mirror. It made me sensitive and easily hurt by negative remarks. It fooled me into thinking that good grades were all that I had to offer and nothing else was special about me.

It halted me from getting involved in activities like sports and talent shows, or putting myself out there in any situation that involved an audience. I feared not performing well and looking stupid. Insecurity convinced me that the shapeliness of my body was a bad thing since it made me a target for ridicule. It deceived me into thinking that no older person would try to take advantage of my childish ignorance and touch me or talk to me. It didn't make sense that they'd want me instead of other girls. It made me think that I wasn't good enough to be compared to other young girls. My words weren't good enough to be spoken. My songs weren't good enough to be sung or my dances to be danced. My talents—if I had any—weren't good enough to be shared with others. It convinced me that I just wasn't good enough; wasn't special and that maybe, I had no purpose at all.

No matter how beautiful or special my family told me I was, I didn't believe them. My only confidence was that I was smart. No one could convince me otherwise. Every honors assembly, report card, test score and gifted program I participated in was proof.

I knew that at least the praise I received for that tiny aspect of me was genuine. As far as all of the other positive remarks, I figured they felt obligated to say those things because that's what family does.

But, one day, with tears rolling down my cheeks and negativity racking my maturing brain, I stopped and asked myself one very important question, *By whose standards am I deciding that I'm not good enough?*

I realized that the only one who could get those dangerous thoughts out of my head was me. I had to build confidence in myself, accept my flaws and weaknesses and recognize my strengths and beauty, inside and out. I was tired of feeling unhappy with me. I knew I still had a lot of growing up to do, and I did not want to go into high school—the start of my young-adult life—with insecurity polluting my spirit. Through other women, I had observed that insecurity was extremely dangerous if it continued to manifest.

The number-one killer of young women wasn't HPV or HIV/AIDS. The number-one killer of young women is insecurity: the evil root of doubt in women of various ages, sizes and ethnicities. We look at media, advertisements and other women, and then doubt ourselves or believe that we're not good enough. Doubt keeps women in abusive, unfaithful, dishonest and unhealthy relationships. Doubt fails to realize full potential, worth and all their gifts. Doubt ceases to pursue dreams, achieve goals and take chances. Doubt fuels numerous young women to lay precious bodies with someone who does not cherish or respect them, in desperate attempts to find love and acceptance. Doubt leads to heartbreak, negative reputations and sexually transmitted disease. Insecurity ensures that women settle for less than they deserve, going through life regretful or unfulfilled. Insecurity kills the spirit.

I realized that I could not fool around with insecurity because I wanted to LIVE, not just go through life.

Today, I am a strong young woman. When I observe others, I no longer feel inferior or selfishly relate every thought back to myself. Instead, I wonder, *What are the roots of her rich heritage? Does she recognize how beautiful she is? Is she kindhearted? Does she let anyone take advantage of her? Does she need a friend? Is she in a relationship where love and respect are reciprocated? Does she take pride in the way she presents herself as a young woman?*

I also realize how blessed I am. I pray every night for God to take away any and all negative thoughts and help me to be more confident, courageous, understanding and an overall better person. I surround myself with positive spirits who love and respect me because they love and respect themselves (like my very best friend, Lorenzo, and my Aunt Sabrina—they are the two most beautiful souls in my life). I accept my flaws and weaknesses and realize that my weaknesses do not make me weak, they simply make me human. I may be shy at times, but insecurity no longer invades my thoughts. It is something that I have gladly lost.

Dedicated to My Grandfather

By Michael Geter

Wednesday, January 28, 2004 was the worst day of my life. Like most days, I woke up, wishing I didn't have to go to school, but I got dressed anyway. As my mom and I prepared to leave home, we noticed that my grandpa wasn't awake yet. Although this may not sound strange, it really was because my grandfather is up early in the mornings.

When my mom called for him, we thought it was especially strange because he didn't answer. We went to check on him. I walked to the side of the bed and pulled back the covers. I saw the face of death, and it will never get out of my head.

I knew about death, but I was too young to understand what was happening.

The police came. I went to school; however, when I got there, it hit me. I had just lost a loved one. I broke down. I had never felt so much hurt or anger. My grandfather was taken away from me for no reason.

My family was sad, but no one more so than me. As a fourth grader, seeing my grandpa dead in my house, I thought I may go crazy. I must have been a strong kid because I made it through.

At the funeral, I didn't cry because I had already cried away all my tears. But, as they lowered him into the ground, I felt a piece of me going too. For a while, I had a lot of anger. Over the years, I learned how to deal with the anger and grow from it.

This story and my life are dedicated to the memory of my grandfather. I love him very much.

My Loss

By Latasia Holt

I used to be so attached to my emotional side. I cried when someone said something negative to me, when I didn't get my way or just because. I felt as if it was me against the world. I felt as though things were tragic. But, it was just reality hitting, telling me to be strong and that life was just that way.

I asked myself why the world was so cruel to me. Then I realized that this world is filled with millions of people with lots of different personalities. I even prayed to God for a miracle, but He couldn't do for me what I needed to do for myself. I had to build self-confidence and stop listening to negativity. So, if someone said something negative to me, I accepted it as a positive because it made me stronger.

Getting rid of my bad habit was not hard; however, it wasn't easy either. It took time. I am seventeen and it took me from the age of ten to sixteen to get rid of the bad habit of being overly attached to my emotional side.

Every now and then, I wonder about other people's bad habits and what it takes to lose them. I wonder if it had a big impact on their lives and why they hadn't gotten rid of it. When I daydream, I wonder if I will have to overcome other obstacles in the future.

Sometimes, I go to my best friend or ask helpful teachers for encouraging words and advice. Getting rid of this habit was the best thing for me. I am proud of myself, especially in how I conduct myself as a young lady. I thank God daily for believing in me and making me the person I am. I also thank my parents and family for having faith in me and raising me to be the person I have become. Thank you!

Now He's Gone

By Shatora George

He had been around for as long as I could remember; since I was three-years old to be exact. I can say that he was a major part of my life and a positive person. No matter what I was doing, he encouraged me to do my best. I can't go through this whole writing calling him "he" because it feels disrespectful, so I'll address him by name: Clyde.

Clyde was my mom's boyfriend, the only man I remember settling down with. I don't know where to start. If I write about his life and how good a person he was, then this story will never end, so I will fast forward to his death.

Since he was my mother's boyfriend, she lived in his house with JuJu, TeeTee and Shay. I visited on school breaks and sometimes the weekend.

My twelfth birthday was coming up and I wanted to have a sleepover at his house. It's fair to say that I was excited. The day of my party, Clyde checked into a hotel. He didn't want to be at home with all of those girls.

The next day, the police—or whoever comes to your house to say someone died—showed up at my house at 11:23 at night. I wasn't too sure who was at the door, so I woke up my cousin. She opened the door. The big guy invited himself in and then asked if my mother was home. The guy looked like he meant business and from the look on my cousin's face, I knew that something was wrong. I ran to get my mommy.

When my mom came upstairs, she told me to go to the bathroom. As soon as I reached the room, I heard yelling and crying. I ran back in the living room. My cousin grabbed me tightly. I asked her what was wrong. She looked into my eyes and told me that Clyde died of a heart attack. I cried and screamed, wondering why this happened.

I dreaded his funeral. I didn't want to say goodbye. I didn't handle any of it well, not his funeral and not his death. I still miss him.

My Fear

By Tionna Towler

I used to fear high school. When I was in the seventh grade, my teachers told us that high school was tougher than middle school. They told us the teachers were strict and the work was hard. At first, I didn't care about what they had to say, until one of my teachers brought a former student from the high school.

She told us the same things and she told us about the Ohio Graduation Test. She explained that if we didn't pass it, then we wouldn't graduate. She emphasized how important it was to get good grades during our freshmen year and not slack off. She had me worried.

Eighth grade was the year when everyone focused on us because we were the oldest in the new building. Everything was new. We were the first to graduate from the new building and we were the first to have the new uniforms. It was like our senior year of middle school.

At first, the year went by easily and everything was good. Toward the middle of the year, high-school juniors came to our school and separated us into groups. Each group had two leaders who mentored us. They gave us a tour of the high school. It seemed nice, but I still had my doubts. We also toured the Career Technology Center. I really liked that school, but we couldn't go there until junior year.

When our eighth-grade year was over, I wanted my summer to last forever. I didn't want to be a freshman. I was scared that I would be an outcast or that I'd be picked on because I was a ninth grader. When it was time to get our schedules, we had orientation. We raced to see if we could get to class on time.

The first day of school was chaotic. I didn't know where all of my classes were and the hallways were crowded. Lost! After a few days, I found out that high school was just like middle school, except bigger and with more people. My teachers were nice and the classes were easy. I lost my fears and couldn't wait to be a sophomore.

Grandpa Was a Rolling Stone
By Aleshia Burt

I experienced loss when my Paw-Paw—my grandfather—passed away. He was the best grandpa ever. I loved everything about him. He wanted only the best for my two sisters and me and would have done anything for us.

To be honest, Grandpa was a rolling stone. He had like six wives and lots of children. He was barely in some of his children's lives because he simply had too many.

My Paw-Paw was the first person to give me a one-hundred-dollar bill. He gave it to me right before we went to Disney World. I didn't know how I was going to spend it, but I thought it was the greatest thing ever.

He owned his own restaurant in Indiana and was a very wealthy man. The restaurant was like the one on the show *Happy Days* with the best food. Paw-Paw was a great chef (which runs in the family).

Paw-Paw had bad habits. He drank a lot, ate unhealthy foods and smoked. I guess his bad habits led him to his grave. It's so sad. He also had medical problems that kept him in and out of the hospital. When he came home from the hospital, he had medicine that he was supposed to take. He was weak and relied on his wife to help him with his pills, but she did not do her job.

I know I shouldn't hate people, but this woman didn't take care of my Paw-Paw and he suffered because of it. I think she wanted him to suffer. His last wife was very mean. She didn't care for him, and I think that she used him for his money. She dressed like a teenager and had a nose-ring. I ask the Lord for forgiveness every day because I know that I should never hate anyone.

The day after New Year's, we got a call. Paw-Paw was in the hospital. I thought, *What's new?* He was always in the hospital, and we thought it was another one of those times. When my mom asked us if we wanted to visit him in the hospital, we said no because we wanted to sneak our stupid boyfriends over when they left for Indiana. That was the last time I could have seen him. The next month he was hospitalized again, and he didn't make it.

When we got the call that he was very ill, we prepared to make the short drive from Michigan to Indiana. As we packed, we got another call. He couldn't be revived and my whole world turned upside down.

Loss of My Former Self

By Darnell Edwards

I'm losing myself. I've been losing myself thanks to all the instability this year. I've always been lazy, but this year, my senior year, has gotten out of control. I've always been a little unwilling and lazy to do many things. I didn't want to write this paper. I don't even want to be in school. I wish I were at home, warm, sleeping peacefully in my bed, cuddled up next to Cara or Tyesha.

It seems like I've been at this point of loss since before I can remember. Actually, it was sometime toward the beginning of senior year. So much to do, so many applications, so many papers to fill out, having to go here and there. And everything else. Mostly, it's because of all this college stuff. I've been slowly trying to find out what I wanted to study when I went off to college. I've always been ahead of the game, but I just can't seem to put my finger on it. I want to study so many things: computers, cars, music, video games, any and everything.

I'm usually a self-motivated person. But this year, my motivation comes and goes. Some mornings, I wake up feeling as if I can have the world, others, I know I'm not doing anything. I'm not an early-morning person, so waking up at six or six-thirty keeps me at a distance.

Lastly, as this year has passed by, I seem to be slowly losing friends. I can't relate to some of the friends that I had previously. I guess as people grow up, they may grow apart. Some make bad choices. A few of my friends have made some mistakes that left me wondering why. Especially when they knew that they wouldn't get away with it.

Most of this low motivation revolves around the fact that I stopped caring about many things. Not caring is the biggest reason I feel like I'm losing myself. I just don't care anymore. Or maybe I'm just tired. It could be a little of both. In any case, the person I was is gone.

Letting Go

By Chaelyn Allen

I lost my cousin. She was one of the funniest people I have ever known. She was always so full of life and everyone loved her. We didn't know she would leave us so soon.

She taught me how to swim the summer of seventh grade when we visited her in Minnesota. I wasn't very tall so my younger cousin and I clung onto the wall in the five-foot section of the pool. I tried to hold on to her legs, but she told me that I would never learn how to swim or do anything if I depended on people.

That was the secret of her success: she knew how to be independent. I want to be like her one day. I wish I could tell her that I was accepted into Purdue University—her alma mater. She would have been happy to hear that.

I still have sad moments because everything reminds me of her. When I go to the mall, I see clothes that she would have worn. She was such a fashionista. When I turn on the television, I hear the word "joy." Her name was Joi. I can't get a break! Don't get me wrong. I don't want to forget her or pretend she isn't gone. I just want to escape so I can have one minute to cope.

I don't know how to overcome this hurt. Only four months have passed since she died in October 2010. I'm afraid that letting go of last year and trying to live in this year will be like letting go of her. I don't want to do that. It's hard to know the right thing to do. Hopefully, time will tell.

A Kingdom Waiting: Loss, Triumph and the Young Spirit

To All My Wonderful Grandmas in Heaven

By Ciera Avery

Dear Grandma Shirley, Jewel and Pearley,

This letter is to all of you because I know that you are together in the same place, smiling.

When I think of you, Grandma Jewel, I feel cheated. You left me when I was only four and couldn't grasp the concept of death. Mommy says that I cried every day when we went to your house and I realized you were missing. I know I stayed at your house almost every day since I was a small child, but I don't remember. I have just three memories of you. One is eating red Skittles with you and Janaé before we took a picture. We were all dressed in pink. Another memory is running to your hospital room with all the other kids in the family before you passed. My last memory was after you passed. I didn't understand how I could see you on the TV in a family video, but could no longer touch you or visit you. Too much for a four-year-old to figure out, I guess. When I was twelve or so, Mommy and I were in the living room talking about you. I got a little sad and went to my room to cry. My tears came because I missed you and I longed to know you more. I still do.

Great Grandma Pearley! My best memories of you were in that nursing home. Although I hated the smell of that place, I dealt with it because I loved to see you. You were so funny and so real. Your stories painted such vivid pictures of family experiences that when I see these people at family gatherings, I thought about your stories. Your hair was so long and beautiful, its color so rich and luxurious. Mommy sometimes compares my hair to yours when it's having a good day. But on a more serious note, I miss you like crazy.

Although I was young, I understood and appreciated you. I wish I had just a little more time with you. When we got the news of your passing, Mommy, Janaé and I were riding in the car and Beyonce's song, *Resentment,* was playing. That song now reminds me of you and forever will.

Grandma Shirley! Because it's still fresh, I can't grasp the fact that you're gone. You're the grandma I spent the most time with, and I enjoyed every moment of it. I loved your strong personality, your style, sweetness and all your personal sound effects. I remember when Mommy, Janaé and I came over to go to church with Paw-Paw. I changed my mind because my hair was so nappy. Do you remember what you said to me? You said, "Baby, you're beautiful but…you do need a perm." I laughed so hard that day. You always reassured us that we were beautiful and special. I miss the sense of self-worth and security you gave me. I remember the call that started it all. Paw-Paw called me and said that you didn't seem right. We rushed you to the hospital. The rest was an emotional roller coaster that none of us could stop. One day you told me that there was nothing we could do at this time. It broke my heart to hear you say that because I would have given anything to get you out of that bed and make you well. I stayed in that hospital with you every day I could, even when that meant not changing clothes and having my cheerleading coach drop me off at the hospital after practice. Your funeral seemed unreal. We sat in the front row as everyone hugged and consoled us. You were ours and no one could ever fill your shoes, Grandma.

To all my wonderful grandmas in Heaven, I miss you more than words could ever express. I know you are in a more beautiful place. My prayer is that one day we can all reunite and then I can have endless, loving Grandma kisses.

Love,
Ciera

Never Judge a Book by Its Cover

By Jamae Finch

I am a living example of the saying that you can never judge a book by its cover. To look at me, you would never imagine the many things I've been through. Most people only see a kind face and happy demeanor. But underneath, things are not nearly so pleasant.

My mother was born and raised in Dayton, Ohio. She moved to Norfolk, Virginia with my father, who was military. They had been together a while when I was born. I've been told that my father denied me as his daughter and that angered my mother. Eventually, my parents went their separate ways. My mother met a new man and later had my sister. Once they were married, we were one happy family: mother, father, two children and a nice home. As far as I knew, I lived with both of my parents, and it seemed like nothing could go wrong.

Being young made it hard to understand many things including how such a happy family could fall apart. I remember waking to yelling and screaming. I ran, jumped in the middle to try to break it up and then my hair got pulled. Crazy. I was only five and I guess I felt as though it was my duty to try to fix things. The police came to our home to discuss the problems. Watching my sister cry because she was scared was hard, but I couldn't cry. I just knew that it was going to get better and everything would be okay again.

To get away from the drama of our dad, my mother kept us living in hotels for the next few years. Some of them were good; we had friends and support systems. Some of them were bad. Like in one, my mom found a babysitter who seemed nice; however, this babysitter and her family abused me. They handcuffed me and laughed while I tried to free myself. Sometimes, they starved me. I remember one of them picked me up and then dropped me on the hard floor. They kept me from using the restroom which eventually affected my bladder. This experience hurt my self-esteem.

When my mother found out, she snatched me away from the situation, but the damage to my self-worth had been done. I think I let the abuse go on for so long without saying something because I thought I deserved it. I was angry, too. I had hard feelings toward my sister because she didn't have my back. She went along with it the whole time. For a short while, I hated my sister. No one knew because I had learned to deal with it by hiding my pain. I felt alone.

Eventually, we found a house and I loved it. Things were stable for a while. I made many friends. I liked my school. I had one close friend who lived across the street. Although things weren't perfect, they were much better.

Then I got strange news from my mother. She told me that my father contacted my grandma because he was looking for us. He wanted to meet me. I didn't understand. As far as I knew, I had a dad and even though he wasn't always there, I loved him very much. I denied the possibility of having a new father. I felt ashamed that the person I called daddy wasn't really my dad.

I was shocked to meet my real dad. To my surprise, I looked just like him. I thought he was so cool. He had a dog, a computer, a truck and a nice house. Back then, that's all it took to impress me.

I remember my first Christmas with my new daddy and sisters. I met my oldest sister and her daughter—my niece. I met two other sisters who came from out of town. We spent the whole break together creating memories. I finally knew my family. I put our t-shirts on his (now "our") dog and dressed my niece like a boy. The best time ever. They not only accepted and loved me, but they loved my sister equally. He was not only a father to me, but to her as well.

Then I found out we were moving to Ohio. I loved Ohio, but I didn't want to pick up and go. We had moved so many times—and I got over it—but this move was the scariest. We didn't even get to say goodbye to anyone. The ride home was fun, but when the trip was over, I was in a new place. The snow was as high as my knees and everything else was just as different.

We had to wear uniforms at my new school. The kids teased me about the gap in my teeth and my lisp. Despite the hard adjustments, this school system helped me cope with my insecurities because it was the only one I attended for more than a year. By the time I learned to express my feelings and think more of myself, my world turned upside down yet again.

My real daddy called to tell me that he had cancer. I couldn't believe it. I'd never seen happy endings when it came to cancer, so I was frightened. As time went by, I accepted that he was sick because I convinced myself that everything would be fine. That's what he told me, so I believed him. I loved him even though he wasn't always there. When he was there, he was a great father and made up for the missed time.

Then I heard my sister speak words that I will never forget. "Jamae, Daddy's gone." My heart dropped. It couldn't be true. I wasn't ready. We had so many father/daughter things to do. I wanted him to see me graduate. Those dreams were gone and I was left with nothing but memories. The only pictures I had are mental images which became blurry and hard to keep fresh over time.

One of the worst parts about his passing is the guilt I have over my last days with him. Though I was happy to see him, he looked miserable and in pain. I decided to spend time with the man who was father to me before I knew my real dad. I cut the visit with my dying father short to see the one who raised me. But when I was there, they treated me like a stranger. He acted like I wasn't his daughter. The pain of his rejection was deep. I was furious because that time was the last one I had with my real daddy. I blame myself for making such a stupid decision. It affected my whole life.

I hate time because it takes me further and further away from when everything was perfect. I used to have two fathers, and now I have none. One left without a choice. One left because I just wasn't important enough. No matter how much I loved him, I was only his daughter's half sister—his stepdaughter—who held no importance. The rejection almost killed me. I had no answers. I was at a loss about how to feel.

Today, I am able to look myself in the mirror. I've learned to accept that although I'm not the prettiest in the bunch, I am a wonderful person. Even though I've had much rejection, I still have many people who enjoy the person I am. I'm still young. I will continue to learn to love myself and attack this complicated life one step at a time.

You Never Know What You Have

By Precious Carmichael

One major loss I've suffered was my boyfriend. He was my first love, my everything; from my best friend to my lover. I trusted him with everything, never held a single thing back. I thought we'd be together for the rest of my life. Then, he took away his love.

Now, I hold back. I don't trust a soul. I'm just not secure about loving again. He was the first person to break my heart. It felt horrible. His past kept him from fully trusting me. Well, I also gave him reasons not to trust me. I regret everything I ever said or did to make him doubt me. But, he has to understand that he hurt me. I expected him to treat me like he treated his past girlfriends but instead, he treated me great. The problem: I thought it was too good to be true. I guess you never know what you have until it is gone. I just wish I could have believed and trusted him.

We still talk. Maybe we will get back together. If he comes back to me after all this hurt, I know that it's true love. I miss him. I want him back, but if not, then I will have to move past him and move on with my life. I love him and always will. I just need to learn to forgive, even though I can't forget.

Emotionally Missing

By Brandon Davenport

To lose something is to lose a part of who you are. Many people believe that I have a perfect life—and I mostly do—aside from the one thing I lost which changed who I am forever. That thing: my father.

When I was little, I didn't realize I didn't have a father. I had my granddad, uncles and many other people to fill that void. I had someone to do everything with me and I had no reason to complain. For years, I never thought of my dad. Every month we got a check from some man I didn't know—free money—so I lived any little boy's dream with all the things I wanted.

As I got older, I felt the absence of my father, but I didn't want to acknowledge it. Every day, I felt something missing. It ate at my emotions slowly. Some days my emotions were so drained that I was sad and unable to focus. However, when people asked me what was wrong, I said, "Nothing." I was taught to not wear my emotions on my sleeve. Also, I didn't want to mention my father because I didn't want to upset my mother. I thought she would feel like she let me down. I didn't want her to think it was her fault that I didn't know my dad. That couldn't be further from the truth.

In the back of my mind, I wanted to know him, but didn't know how to go about it. At times, I thought that next year my dad would show up to meet me. It never happened. My whole life I tried to do everything perfect because I thought it would bring my father to me. I worked extra hard in school, even skipped a grade, hoping to give him more reason to come back.

I continued this trend of hard work and hoping for Daddy

until I was twelve. It was Father's Day and I had absolutely nothing to do. My granddad was out of town. All my friends were with their dads. Even my sister was spending the weekend with her father. I was home by myself, and I decided that I was going to find my dad.

I packed some clothes and walked to the bus stop to find my dad. I was too young to get on the bus by myself, so I went back home. I decided to look for him on the computer. I searched his name, but hundreds of people had his name, so that plan failed. I turned on the television and every show was about dads. I couldn't watch anymore. I cut it off, went to my room and found a check from my dad on the dresser. My mom forgot to put it away. With the check in my hand, I sat on the floor in my room. I wondered about this mysterious man and how my life would be with him in it.

I concluded that I would never meet him and the hurt took over my heart. I couldn't handle it, so I cried. I cried for an hour or two until I had no more tears. I told myself that I needed to grow up, deal with this inevitable fact and get over myself. I didn't see any point in telling anyone about it, so I didn't. I never felt anything close to that pain again. That was the last time I cried.

Since then, my life has been better. I have done better and will become more successful without my father. Maybe my life will be better with him in it, but I guess I will never know. And I am okay without knowing. As the poet, Thomas Gray, said, "Ignorance is bliss." That is exactly what I need to remember to make the best of my life. I still think about him, but not as much as I used to. I think it is normal, but I won't let it take over my life. Hey, maybe he will buy this book, read it and find me, but if that never happens, I have learned that it does not matter what you lose or think you have lost, just make the best of your situation.

Trust

By Kenny Cochran

In my eighteen years of life, I have encountered much pain, struggle and loss. The largest loss—or the one that sticks out to me the most—is when my parents separated. I was in the eighth grade and had no idea how serious the separation was. Even though my father moved to Miamisburg, I still had hope that he would move back home. After the move, my father often came back to our house which caused huge arguments between him and my mother. Tears were in my eyes many nights before I went to sleep.

Around the time of the separation, I lost my relationship with my father. Every time I forgave him for disrespecting my mother, something happened to put me back in "hate mood." My father has a heart of gold and would give his last dime to a stranger. And although this trait is wonderful, I think it's one of his largest flaws. I say this because he would spend all of his money to help a friend and then fall short to provide his own needs.

Marriage has no meaning to me. Almost every marriage I have witnessed has ended. I was often told "Mommy and Daddy will work out our issues and things will get better." Four years later, the situation is worse. I don't want to blame my parents' marriage for my issues, but I think it's a big reason why I don't trust anyone. I had a woman who loved me unconditionally and would do anything for me. I loved her, too, but at times, I acted as if I didn't. My unfaithful actions—due to trust issues that grew from my childhood experiences—brought our relationship to a halt. In hindsight to that relationship, I would do anything to get that love back, but I know that I have to take the relationship with her as a great loss.

After all of these years, after all the tears and all the terrible memories, I just want to have a family again. Not a family who gets along seasonally, but a family who truly loves each other through harsh winters and sizzling summers. I have a relationship with my father, but I lost the genuine one I had with him when I was younger. As a result, I am working on trusting people. All the females whom I have blatantly disrespected, I feel their pain and truly apologize. Lack of trust, infidelity, drugs, money, selfishness and lack of support are just a few elements that can destroy a relationship. Each one of them contributed to my loss of relationships.

A Letter to Myself

By Elisha Street

Dear Street,

How are you? Don't say that you're good because you know you're not. You've completely shut me out of your life. You have me locked away in this cage and won't let me out. Why have you become this person? Why do you do the things you do? I know, but you don't.

You have no feelings—well, at least that's what you've convinced yourself to believe. You've convinced yourself to have the wrong mentality. It's sad to see you hurt yourself this way. How did you become this person? When and where did it all start?

You used to be a distinguished individual; you didn't care what people thought about you. You were happy! But, all you do now is hurt. You are quick to anger, easy to forgive and you give everyone the benefit of the doubt. That is your downfall! Your kindness is your weakness and people take advantage of that. Well, let me say that it is not you they take advantage of, Street; it is me, Elisha.

You don't care about anything. You say forget men and everyone else because you trust no one, especially men. You've given them your heart, and they did nothing but destroy it. They've broken it; they've repaired it, but you've yet to find anyone who will protect it. You say it doesn't bother you, but deep down, you're hurting inside.

You, not I, can do things and have no emotions after. I used to say that I was going to wait until marriage to have sex, but you broke that promise. Most girls get attached to the man who takes their virginity, but not you. You felt nothing. Emotionless. Your heart is scarred beyond its years.

It's like a dry piece of clay that needs the potter to add moisture on it and finish shaping it.

You do things that hurt to feed the pain inside. You bruise your body, and you don't even feel the pain. Pain is all you ever felt, so how can it hurt you?

Mom asked you why you do the things you do. You told her that you didn't know, but Mom knows. She said that you want a daddy and look for males to give you the attention that only a father can give to his little girl.

You are a broken China doll who seems unable to be fixed. You have such low self-esteem. You don't think you're pretty. You *are* beautiful. People tell you that, but you don't believe them. You are so empty. It feels like you don't have a heart. It's as if a hard rock has taken its place. You have a lonely soul. Sometimes you want to cry, but the tears just won't come. You need help because you're dying inside.

You desire to be wanted and loved, but no one wants you—at least that's what you think. I'm writing you this letter because I love you. I know you. You won't read it because it's not meant to be sent. I keep knocking on your door, but you refuse to answer.

Sincerely,
Elisha

My G-Mom

By Alexis Davis

One day, my sister told me that she and my dad were coming to pick me up to take me to my great-grandmother's house. I didn't want to go because I had just seen my great-grandmother that Saturday when my granduncle came to fix the garage door. I loved my great-grandmother, but I just didn't feel like going over there that day. My sister told me to call my mom after I hung up with her. I called my mom. She said that I wasn't going to my soccer game.

My great-grandmother died in the fall of 2010. I was three years old when she was diagnosed with Alzheimer's disease in 1995. My G-Mom, as she liked to be called, was known to play favorites, and I was her favorite. She picked me up for a day, and we would be gone for a week. If I needed new shoes, she took me to the store, and I got a completely new outfit. I wanted for nothing.

My great-grandmother was the one who piqued my interest in the library and reading. I don't have a lot of vivid memories of those times because I was so young.

When I was in my teens, she came to visit. I was kind of afraid of her because she couldn't remember me or anyone else. She asked me who I was so many times that I gave other answers (everyone did at some point or another). I said that I was my sister, my cousin or my mom on occasion. I didn't do it often, just when she asked who I was five, six, seven times in a row.

I stayed away from her during social gatherings. How are you supposed to act around an older lady—a great-grandparent—who acts like a baby? When she was in her more lucid state, I talked to her without being nervous. But when the disease worsened, she didn't speak much. When she did speak, she whispered. You had to stand close to her to hear what she said. Sometimes when she talked, it didn't make any sense. Other times, she recalled a distant memory, and I wouldn't have a clue as to what she was talking about.

After she was diagnosed, I learned a lot about Alzheimer's disease. It is a neurological disease that affects many Americans with effects varying from person to person. It takes an emotional toll on the caretakers, especially if they are related. My grandfather moved into my great-grandmother's house to help take care of her. My granduncle also came by to help.

She had to be watched all the time or she would get into trouble. In the early stages, she asked to go home, even if she was at home. She walked away, and then you had to catch her and put her back in her seat. As the disease progressed, she behaved more outlandishly. Whatever her hands touched, she put in her mouth and tried to eat. My grandfather said that he caught her eating soap and a napkin.

Her health took a turn for the worse. In the last few months, she wouldn't eat willingly so we had to force her to eat. The doctor said that her time was close, so my granduncle had her eulogy written. She was in and out of the hospital as well as the nursing home. She had gotten skinnier and skinnier, until she was literally skin and bones.

Even though she was sick, she was as stubborn as she wanted to be. If you tried to give her a hug, she turned away from you, as much as she could, anyway. The fire and defiance in her eyes were obvious when someone made her do something she didn't want to do. She looked like death. Sometimes she slept and did not respond to attempts to wake her. My mother said that my G-Mom knew she was going to die. She thought that was one reason she didn't want to eat anymore: My G-Mom was ready for death.

After she died, my family went to her house to remember her life. By the time we arrived at her house, Wright-Patt had already collected her body. I couldn't remember much of our time together, but it was nice to hear the stories. We looked through several photo albums she had around the house and retold stories of what was happening while the picture was being taken. Some pictures were funny, others were confusing and some were just sad.

We didn't have a funeral because she donated her body to science when she was in her right mind. I'm happy for it. I don't like funerals and people crying. I don't believe she did either.

Having a great-grandparent with Alzheimer's disease taught me a lot about myself. I thought I could handle the sick or mentally challenged. I thought that even with the disease, I could behave normally and talk to them like normal human beings. But, I was scared of my own G-Mom. I didn't want to be the person to feed or bathe her.

I hope that something like that never happens to me or anyone else in my family. I don't think I could handle it. Individuals with this type of disease aren't contagious, and it's not their fault. They still want to be talked to and taken care of, but I couldn't believe how someone so independent could revert to behaving like a child. I felt inferior. I sat back and watched my family take care of my great-grandmother. My little sister and younger cousins talked to her, fed her, even bathed her without thinking twice. I wondered why I couldn't do the same. I loved my great-grandmother and I would do anything for her, but I couldn't handle taking care of her when she was sick.

I have a lot of growing up to do. If my grandparents or parents fall sick, I want to be able to take care of them. Likewise, if I ever have children and grandchildren, I want them to take care of me. I don't want them to drop me off at a nursing home and forget about me. I feel that I wronged my great-grandmother because I didn't want to be around her. I hope she can forgive me, and I'm sorry it took her death to make me realize it.

Loss of a Father, Growth of a Child

By Desiaire Rickman

I was born Desiaire Rickman to a man and woman who were in a less-than-stable relationship. At an early age, it was obvious that I was a bright child. My father sat me down and taught me the basics of learning. By the time I was in kindergarten, I read and wrote at a third-grade level. I spoke with intelligence beyond my time. Teachers were awed and amazed when I was placed in their classes. As I grew educationally, my sister and brother were born; one year and six years after me, respectively. My first responsibility: be a good sister and role model to my siblings. So I was. I looked out for them. I gave them attention when they needed it or when my parents couldn't give it to them. I did what I had to do, and it made me a better person. However, with this heavy responsibility, I couldn't be a child.

At about six-and-a-half-years old, I sat on my loving father's lap. He held a map in front of us to study the geography of the United States of America. We laughed and smiled. I enjoyed daddy-and-daughter time—one of the best and most precious times in the world. Our picture-perfect setting was interrupted by a loud noise. Lights flashed and sirens thundered as our front door crashed to the floor. Two police officers entered. One pointed a gun at my father, and the other snatched me from his hands. I cried and screamed and begged the officers to leave my daddy alone. They handcuffed him and forced him out of the house.

With my brother and sister in her arms, my mother ran to me. She took us into another room, turned on the television and then put *The Lion King* in the DVD player. She closed the door and then ran after my daddy. I cradled my brother and sister as my parents traded words; harsher than ever before. Apparently, he had committed yet another crime. Tears streamed down my cheeks as I heard the sirens fade away; the blue and red lights eventually overshadowed by the darkness. As I held my siblings tightly, I locked away my tears and held my quivering chin high.

My mother's face echoed my own, her spine steel-rod straight. Nothing ever seems to break her. I admire her for it.

Things settled down, and my expectations grew even steeper. With my father gone, my mother relied on me to take care of the house and my siblings. She had to work since our father's income was gone. I watched them, played with them, fed them, clothed my baby brother and made sure both were bathed. I got my sister and myself to school while my mother looked after my brother. For a few months, everything was quiet; then my father came home.

He picked up teaching me. Nothing major happened. My parents kept quiet—for which I am grateful—but then my father started coming home later and later. (I learned later that he had another family. I was an aunt to my half-sister's kids.) The fights resumed between my parents, until my father took it too far. He threatened to take us away so my mother wouldn't ever see us again. My mom lost it, but instead of going berserk, she got smart.

She packed our things and moved us from our Virginian land to the bustling city of Dallas, Texas. We lived there for ten years. As I got older and smarter, my responsibilities increased with chores, homework and of course, big-sister duty. The activities kept me from being active and social, so I grew into a shy and slightly awkward girl. I stayed quiet and never became involved in a serious relationship with any guy. My mother didn't want me involved with boys and memories of my parents' relationship left me wary.

After I turned sixteen, we left Dallas to move to Trotwood, Ohio. Family brought us back to my mother's native state and the new surroundings inspired a change in my character. For good? For bad? Maybe. Depends on who you ask. I met amazing friends who loved me for me and didn't expect anything in return. For that I was grateful. But I didn't want to relive the pain that my father inadvertently placed on me, so I didn't allow myself to get close to any guy. That is until I met my best friend, Julian, through a school program. We exchanged numbers and with our first conversation, we became best friends. I've never been as close to a person of the opposite sex as I am with him. I love him for finally breaking the impenetrable barrier that I had built around my heart.

Some people may recount the loss of a father by trying to present him in the best of lights. However, I do it straight-cut. My father was not a good man, but he was a good father when he wanted to be. Had I not lost my father, I wouldn't have found my inner strength: strength of a child; strength of a woman. Loss can hurt and it can heal. Loss can change a person and it can lead to new truths. I grieved for my father for so long and grieved even more for my mother. I never took the time to grieve for myself. I have learned to do that and now I am able to let go.

My father was recently released from prison for the crime he committed, the one that gave my mother the chance to escape. I've spoken to him, even called him Dad. I respect him for the father he was, but it'll be a long time before I respect him for the man he is. I only hold respect for one man, my best friend. But as time moves forward, I know that this great loss will present greater opportunities.

Thanks, Dad. Losing you was the best thing that ever happened to me.

Losing Myself in Shadows

By Ebony Munday

When I hear the word "loss," I think of unattainable love or the death of someone close. It's not often that I talk about what I wish I could have lost. So why not give it a shot? I have a tremendous fear which I yearn to overcome. I, Ebony Angelina Munday, am petrified of the dark.

This fear is not as juvenile as you may think. Most people are under the impression that fearing the dark is about monsters or the result of watching horror movies. My fear is more spiritually based. I am a proud believer of the Christian faith, but something about darkness gives me a rather uneasy feeling. No matter how hard I try, I cannot shake this childhood fear.

My fear surfaces when I am alone. If I can't see any light, paranoia starts and then I panic. Darkness has eyes. The devil does most of his sinister acts in the shadows. Even though I love and trust God, my fear is never-ending.

For seventeen years, religion was the main thing my father instilled in me. With pride, I follow the path of Christ, yet I can't help but be ashamed. I was taught to love, trust and only fear the wrath of God. "No weapon formed against you shall prosper" (Isaiah 54:17). It's hard for me to live by this Scripture because along with God, I also fear Satan. I often ask myself, *How can I fear the good and the bad? Am I lesser in God's eyes because I allow the devil to intimidate me?*

This matter puts a huge burden on my shoulders. My fear of the darkness has affected my life in the most negative ways. For instance, I could be at home or in a public place and feel like I am in danger, if I am in complete darkness.

I've always believed that evil lurks in the dark, waiting to secretly stir trouble. I literally have panic attacks when I'm in my state of paranoia. I feel like I'm losing myself as a person and everything good that I stand for because the scene around me goes blank. My tears show weakness and in my opinion, a Christian is not supposed to be weak.

My daddy taught me that a true Christian does not fear the devil, but rather the devil is supposed to fear and feel threatened by the Christian.

I read about sorrow and darkness or good versus evil in my Advanced Placement English 12 class, and I took much of what we discussed into consideration. Oscar Wilde, for example, spoke of Christ as the reason for living and that earthly sins can lead to sorrow. He even stated that the devil does his best work in the dark by trying to manipulate as many as he can.

I know that this fear is all in my mind, but I still believe all of the old-wives' tales I have heard about the devil. Nevertheless, I can honestly say that God has helped me control my fear of the dark. When I am feeling unbearably afraid at night—regardless of if I have a glimmer of light from my TV—I open my Bible to the book of Psalms and then place it on my headboard. This action gives me a sense of protection.

I do believe that one day this paranoia will subside. I know that God will keep me protected. I just have to have faith and believe that the devil cannot physically harm a child of God because He promised: "No weapon formed against me shall prosper."

The Loss of Trust

By Chrisha Taylor

The loss of trust is almost like the loss of love because it's indescribable. My trust slowly faded away for a few people. It seemed like the worst thing to find out that I was being lied to over and over again. It is terrible to trust someone for so long and then get crushed.

I had a boyfriend whom I trusted. It seemed like nothing could come between us. Little did I know: nothing is impossible. I put my all into the relationship, but I was the only one working hard to keep it together.

And just when I thought I had learned from my mistakes, I figured out that a few of my friends weren't so trustworthy either. Talking behind my back, the smiles and grins that seemed sincere. We did things together on the weekends. They knew my deepest, darkest secrets. It's crazy how easily petty things can come between people and break them apart.

Now I have up a big guard toward everyone, and as much as I want to knock it down, it doesn't work that way. I only trust a few people. It's especially bad because I can't even believe anything my own father says. He can come with all the proof in the world, and I still don't think I could bring myself to believe him. I know that my mother and father should have all of my trust, but I guess it doesn't work that way.

Sometimes people label me as bitter or mean because I don't easily open up and I'm not likely to be friendly. I can't help being so selfish. I never want to be stuck in a bad place. I just can't be betrayed again.

I Will Never Forget

By Shaunice Passmore

Losing someone close creates such grief. The pain, the irony, the sadness, the horror involved in death is often unbearable. When you lose someone close to you, you feel like you've lost yourself in the process. Having someone you're accustomed to seeing every day creates comfort. To not be able to see that person ever again saddens the soul.

I am a victim of just that. I lost my grandmother, my best friend, my second mother, my everything. I knew not to ask God why because my grandma always told me to never question God's work. He knows what He is doing and He never makes mistakes, but many times I did want to ask why. Even now I want to know, but I've been taught better.

My sister said to me, "Not to worry. Everything is going to be all right." I knew I'd be in good hands after my grandmother's death, but I also knew that things would never be the same. I was not ready for the changes to come.

My grandma adopted me when I was eleven-months old and I lived with her until she died. It was not that my mother didn't want me. She just couldn't afford another child living in a home with six other people. My grandma and my mom talked about it and decided that adopting me was the best choice. I saw my mom, brother and Daddy as much as I liked.

I miss my grandmother dearly. I will never forget the memories we shared and the love she brought to me. Although a piece of me is still missing, hopefully, time will heal all.

A Loss of Memory

By Michael Booze

During freshman year, my team played a basketball game against Troy. It was the first quarter and we were winning.

My last memory was going up for a lay-up and then the next thing I knew, I was on a bench. Two trainers and the coach were in front of me, asking questions.

"Do you know where you are? Do you know what happened?" I knew the first answer, but not the second. They told me that I got bridged—that happens when you jump for a lay-up and another player runs under you causing you to flip in the air—but I didn't believe them.

The trainers didn't want me to keep playing. I was sad; sat on the bench, low-key crying because I wanted to get back in the game. I wanted to help my team win. I had to sit out, but we still won.

I took the game film home and was shocked! I really got flipped. I watched it over and over, like thirty times. Amazing! I understood why I didn't remember anything.

After watching the film so many times, I just wanted to go out and play. I could have really been hurt to the point of never being able to play basketball again. My career on the court could have ended and that's when I started to practice as hard as I play. I decided to do that because basketball could be taken from me at any time. I have learned to care for it more. I appreciate what I have.

The Strongest Man I Knew

By Krysta Coleman

I lost my Paw-Paw in 2005. I write about him a lot. I want to make sure that I remember him because he died when I was young. I figure that if I write about him and reread my work, then I'll be able to remember him and reminisce on the times we shared.

He suffered for years. He had poor kidneys and attended dialysis weekly. Although he was internally ill, he didn't let it show. He remained the same man he'd always been.

He still watered Granny's garden and planted vegetables like Brussels sprouts and green tomatoes. Man, he made the best fried green tomatoes and the best desserts. My sister and I begged him to create a recipe book, but he refused.

He took my cousin, D'Angelo, and me out for ice cream one summer afternoon. We had so much fun. We talked and laughed the whole time. That's my favorite memory with him because he showed me that although he was sick, he wouldn't be restrained from spending time with his loved ones.

Paw-Paw got around pretty well, until he started having difficulties. When he was checked into the hospital, the doctors were able to find the problem. Unfortunately, though, his legs needed to be amputated. When I found out that he'd no longer have legs, I was devastated. When I saw him for the first time after his surgery, I didn't know how to react. I wanted to spare him any more heartache, so I fought back my tears until I was out of his sight.

Although Paw-Paw's legs were gone, he refused to let anyone feel sorry for him. He didn't like when people cried because he was ill. He told them, "With or without legs, I'm still Bill."

I admired him for his strength and faith. He knew his time on this earth was almost up, but he didn't allow it to take a toll on him.

The day my father came upstairs to my bedroom to tell me Paw-Paw was gone, I cried until I couldn't cry anymore. I felt as if I'd lost a best friend. I'll never forget that day.

I wish I could get one more chance to see him, just so I could tell him how much I love and miss him. He was the strongest man I knew. And, he will be loved forever.

Swimming

By Auston Smith

Swimming was an obstacle for me because I thought I may drown. I saw someone drown on television. It shocked me and ever since, I've been afraid that it could happen to me.

My brother taught me how to swim last summer. It took about three weeks because I didn't want to put my head under the water. I didn't think I could hold my breath.

I enjoy swimming now. It feels good to swim in any depth of water. I guess you could say that I'm comfortable. I'm glad my fear didn't come true.

I considered joining our school's swim team. The students on the team take swimming very seriously. They are passionate about it. I would love to be a part of that one day, but not now. I'm a good swimmer; however, I want to be a great swimmer before I join a swim team and compete against others.

Learning to swim has always been a goal of mine. Now that I've achieved this goal, I'm proud and happy with myself and my accomplishments.

Achieving my goals has made me more confident that I can achieve anything. If I can overcome a life-long fear, then I can overcome any other obstacle such as grades or playing on the football field. This marks the beginning of a lot of greatness to come.

My Biggest Reality Check

By Jasmine Owensby

December 20, 2010, I had my biggest reality check: I went to my first funeral.

When my Aunt Carrie Raines died, it was a sad and depressing time for me. Many thoughts ran through my mind. *Is this serious? Why didn't Makala tell me? Where have I been?*

My mind was overwhelmed with guilty thoughts. I didn't know how to handle the situation since I had never lost someone I truly cared about, so I cried. At the same time, I was confused. It seemed that my cousin, Makala, had already gotten over the death of her mother.

I asked Makala, "Why didn't you call me? Why are you laughing?" I guess she just realized that her mother was in a better place. I didn't know whether my cousin was crazy or if she really had just gotten over it.

I think about my aunt every day. I wish I would have had the chance to at least say goodbye. I feel guilty because many times I told Makala that I was going to see her mother in the nursing home, but I never did.

I will forever remember the times we shared and the things she said to me. She told me not to eat too much salt or hot sauce because it would catch up to me when I'm older. Her diet is the reason she's no longer here. Her kidneys failed.

I will take what she told me seriously. I will not let her lesson be in vain.

All For the Best

By Kendra Crowe

I lost a relationship with my best friend. I remember it like it was yesterday. She told the class that she was moving and wouldn't come back until fifth grade. I was devastated. I was so young and couldn't understand why she had to move. I tried to move on with my other friends, hoping that she really didn't have to move.

Then the day came when she got all of her stuff from school, and I didn't see her anymore at school. I felt like God didn't like me and there was no point in going to school. It took me a couple of days to accept that she was gone, but eventually, I got over it.

Looking back on it now is funny, but at the time, it seemed like the world had ended.

In the seventh grade, I moved to Trotwood. I walked into class and there she was, talking to some people.

I walked over to her and said, "Hello."

She asked, "Do I know you?"

I told her about Dayton Catholic. She remembered me, but I felt like she didn't like me anymore. I tried being friends with her. I acted like her current friends. I talked to the same people. But for some reason, I kept attracting people she and her friends thought were lame. They even called me lame which basically labeled me as such: the lame new kid.

She was popular, so she just stopped talking to me and then I stopped talking to her. The friendship was dead. I hoped for a long time that the relationship could be fixed, but I realized that it could not.

I wonder if the friendship was formed again, who would I be. Some things are not meant to be known. It may be good that she and I are no longer friends. I found out that she is an ignorant, selfish, unkind person. It was all for the best.

That Will Never Be Me

By Tonisha Williamson

I was a girl who often said, "That will never be me." Now, I see reality and truth. I feel hurt, pain and negative feelings.

The negative feelings came from a person who was not ready to be faithful, true, loyal or respectful. He was scared of love. He had been betrayed and had stared death in the face. He had experienced heartbreak. All of that can take a toll on a person, and it certainly did with him.

When we first met, I said that I would never mess with him or someone like him; however, he got me. We were together and from that day on, drama and lies followed. I swore that I would never put up with cheating and betrayal, but I did.

Abuse was a factor in our relationship: emotional abuse. He said things like, "You will never be anything" and "Nobody will ever want you." He treated me like an object and after a while—although I knew that I was worth more—I started to believe him. His words made me question where it was coming from and how he felt about me. Why was I in love with a person who was so scared of love that he showed his feelings by hurting others?

I said that would never be me. I would not have a guy mistreat or disrespect me. In the end, I was exactly what I said I would not be: someone who put up with lies and cheating.

Being that girl was terrible. I hope I will never go back so that I can truthfully say, "That will never be me."

The Burden of Betrayal

By Brytni Morris

Even though I am still young, I have experienced many trials. One such trial was having my trust betrayed. I learned that I don't have enough boundaries.

I will always love my dad, but he lost my trust when he broke three promises to me. He swore that we'd go out and have family days, but when the weekends came around, he had something else to say.

"I'm sorry, Baby. I have something else to do. I forgot we made plans."

After the first couple of times, I stopped believing the lies and lost all my trust. I reasoned that if he lied about this, he had likely lied to me about many other things.

I'm still working on solving this issue. So far, to help myself through, I set the boundary of not accepting promises from him. I even told him to never make a promise to me again. Although it's not the best solution, at least the problem of being lied to is solved.

It takes time to rebuild trust in *all* relationships once trust is gone in any one relationship. It's important to be honest and share how you feel with the people who are important to you. If you hold things in, you may be setting yourself up for hard times.

I felt like I was being crushed under the burden of it all. But once I shared my feelings, the weight lifted off of my shoulders.

Best Friends, Like Sisters

By Brandee Femuels

Jefferson Montessori Elementary is where it all started. I registered a week late due to a move across town. As my mom and I were checking in with the school secretary, another girl walked up with her father to register. She stood about 4'11" with short hair that sported a blue bow. She looked at me like she knew me, but I had never seen her before.

The secretary asked, "Are you sisters?"

"No!" We both yelled like we hated each other. The secretary laughed.

Mrs. Sadler was my fourth-grade teacher. My assigned seat was near the window, lined with all of her old, dried up plants. The empty desk beside me was occupied later that day by the same girl I met in the office. Mrs. Sadler introduced her to the class as D'Ambre Henderson.

On the way to art class a few minutes later, the other students asked if we were sisters. After a while, we just stopped answering and took seats next to each other.

The teacher noticed we were new and asked, "Are you girls sisters?"

We paused, looked at each other and laughed. When we answered "No" in stereo, we smiled and giggled. In the midst of our art project, I introduced myself. From that moment on, we were inseparable.

She became my best friend. More than friends, we were, ironically, like the sisters that everyone assumed we were.

By seventh grade, fate separated us. D'Ambre left Jefferson. We called each other here and there, but it just wasn't the same. After a while, I didn't hear from her, so I moved on. I met new people and gained new friends.

When high school came, I was once again the new kid who didn't know anyone. The isolation caused me to reconnect with D'Ambre. I went to the movies with her and it was like old times. This was to be the last time I would see her, though. The next time I tried to call her, her phone was disconnected. When I drove by her house, my heart sank. Boxes filled with her bed spread, covers, bags and other personal items were on the side of the road. The garage was empty.

I lost my best friend, again. Memories of us flashed through my head. I stood in the driveway and cried. I didn't know where I could find her.

I now have a new best friend, but I still think about D'Ambre and what I would say if I saw her again. Until then, I'm going to live my life. I never knew that high school could change everything.

Lesson Learned

By Asia Buycks

I never thought I'd be the girl who lost the one person she truly loved and cared about. I thought I would never get over it. I thought it was the end of my life and I would never love again. It was the worst feeling ever. I never felt so much pain at one time.

It felt like my world was crashing around me. I didn't want to talk to anyone. I just wanted to be alone. I didn't even want my phone on or near me. That's how I knew something was really wrong with me.

I could barely talk without shedding a tear or stuttering. I didn't want to go out with my friends. I just wanted to stay in the house and cry.

I kept saying, "Why does it hurt so bad? I never felt this way before. Why me of all people?"

Everybody kept telling me that it was going to be okay which only made me cry and feel worse. Why would anybody hurt the person whom they claimed to love?

It took me a while, but eventually, I did get over it. I realized that it wasn't worth all of the stress. I also knew that he wasn't doing the same. He had obviously moved on, so why couldn't I?

I realized that I wasted my time crying over him. I could have been out partying and having fun instead of trying to be tied down as a teenager. So, I just worried about me and no one else.

I finally talked to him to get closure. He wasn't the one for me after all. I knew that I could do much better.

I kicked myself for crying over him, wasting myself and my time when I could be out enjoying my teenage years.

I have learned my lesson. Never again will I put myself in that type of situation. I am most important. I will always treat myself like I come first because I do.

About the Contributors

Sarah Acton is an alumnus of Kent State University. She graduated Magna Cum Laude in 1999 with a Bachelor of Arts in English. Her honors college thesis—*Branches without Roots: Modern-Day Slaves in Toni Morrison's Trilogy*—was published in 1999 and is housed at the Kent State University Library. She completed a teaching certification program with Wittenberg University in 2002. She has been teaching Language Arts at the secondary level for nine years. Trotwood-Madison High School has been her home for the last eight years, where she has taught Honors English 11, Advanced Placement English 12 and Creative Writing. She is also the English Department Chair and the school's Academic Team Coach. In 2010, she completed her Master of English with a specialty in writing at the University of Dayton. Her Master Thesis—*Jesus' Prison: A Novel*—was published online with OhioLink in 2010. She loves to write in her spare time. She lives in Springfield, Ohio with her husband, Brian, and their daughter, Emry.

Chaelyn Allen is a 2011 graduate of Trotwood-Madison High School. She will attend Purdue University, but is undecided as to her major. She enjoys cheerleading and shopping.

Ciera Avery is a 2011 graduate of Trotwood-Madison High School. She wants to attend Northern Kentucky University to pursue her goal of being a pediatrician. She is a cheerleader and mentor and will continue writing beyond high school.

Korey Beavers is a 2011 graduate of Trotwood-Madison High School. He will attend Mount Vernon Nazarene University to study Ministry. He participates in mock trial and basketball and loves to read the Bible. He plans to continue writing after high school.

Michael Booze is a 2011 graduate of Trotwood-Madison High School. Although he is undecided as to which institute of higher learning he will attend, he will study Sports Medicine and will continue playing basketball. He plans to continue writing for personal enjoyment.

Aleshia Burt graduates from Trotwood-Madison High School in 2012. She will study Forensics at the post-secondary level. She is a busy, energetic young lady who loves to exercise, write poetry and be with family and friends.

Asia Buycks is a member of Trotwood-Madison's class of 2011. After high school, she will pursue a career in nursing. Though she plans on starting at Sinclair Community College, she wants to transfer to a four-year university.

Precious Carmichael is a member of Trotwood-Madison's class of 2013.

Kenny Cochran is a 2011 graduate of Trotwood-Madison High School. He will attend Northern Kentucky University to pursue a career in Psychology. He loves to play sports and wants to write motivational books.

Krysta Coleman is a member of Trotwood-Madison's class of 2013. She plans to double major in Athletic Training and Accounting. She plays volleyball, softball and bowling. She also enjoys dance and hopes to write a book.

Kendra Crowe is a 2011 graduate of Trotwood-Madison High School. She will attend Sinclair Community College to study Business Management and Culinary Arts. She will pursue her love of writing in college and beyond.

Brandon Davenport is a 2011 graduate of Trotwood-Madison High School. He is going to attend Miami

University at Oxford, Ohio to study Communications and Speech Pathology. He enjoys sports and being with friends.

Taylor Davenport is a 2011 graduate of Trotwood-Madison High School. She will attend the University of Akron to become an occupational therapist. In her free time, she enjoys writing and singing.

Alexis Davis is a 2011 graduate of Trotwood-Madison High School. Although she is undecided about which college she will attend, she wants to study Pre-Med and Business. She enjoys track and field, bowling, soccer, knitting and writing.

Darnell Edwards is a 2011 graduate of Trotwood-Madison High School. He will be attending the University of Toledo. He plans to study Computer Engineering or Pre-Law.

Brandee Femuels will graduate from Trotwood-Madison High School in 2012. She plans to attend Wright State University to pursue a career as an Ultrasound Technician. She enjoys cheerleading.

Jamae Finch is a 2011 graduate of Trotwood-Madison High School. Although she is still undecided as to her post-secondary plans, she will certainly go far with her pursuits, as her high-school participation in cheerleading, mock trial, yearbook, mentoring and student government demonstrate.

Shatora George will graduate from Trotwood-Madison High School in 2013. She wants to attend Tennessee State University to study Child Psychology. She enjoys cheerleading and reading.

Michael Geter is a 2011 graduate of Trotwood-Madison High School. He will attend Northern Kentucky University to study Business Management. He plays football.

Lydia Hanns is a 2011 graduate of Trotwood-Madison High School. She will attend Central State University or the

University of Dayton, studying law, medicine or accounting. She will pursue poetry and non-fiction writing.

LaTasia Holt is a 2011 graduate of Trotwood-Madison High School. She will be attending Northern Kentucky University to study Pre-Med and Pediatrics. She enjoys shopping and will continue writing beyond school.

Bryanna Jackson is a 2011 graduate of Trotwood-Madison High School. She will attend Wright State University to study Nursing. She has participated in JROTC, soccer and basketball. She plans on writing to express her feelings.

Renon Lorenzo is a 2011 graduate of Trotwood-Madison High School. He will attend a four-year college to study drama. He enjoys playing sports and composing music. He also likes poetry, especially spoken word poetry.

Courtney McFadden is a 2011 graduate of Trotwood-Madison High School. She will be attending Wright State University to study Nursing and Communications. Her interests include poetry, choir and Spanish.

Brytni Morris is a 2011 graduate of Trotwood-Madison High School. She will attend Sinclair Community College to focus on Communications. She loves to work with animals, write, read and sing. She will continue to write outside of school.

Ebony Munday is a 2011 graduate of Trotwood-Madison High School. She is attending the University of Dayton to pursue Journalism and Communications. She wants to publish fiction.

Jasmine Owensby will graduate from Trotwood-Madison High School in 2013. She is undecided about life after high school, but enjoys dancing.

Shaunice Passmore is a 2011 graduate of Trotwood-Madison High School. She has not yet decided between

Tennessee State University and Howard University, but will study Law and Political Science. She participates in softball and student government.

Maria Rabb will graduate from Trotwood-Madison High School in 2012. She wants to attend the University of San Francisco to pursue a career in Chemical Engineering. She enjoys traveling, art and wants to write children's books.

Desiaire Rickman is a 2011 graduate of Trotwood-Madison High School. She will study Marketing to be a Public Relations Manager. Her hobbies include singing, writing, reading, running and listening to music. Her goal is to write fantasy novels with strong female characters to inspire young girls.

Tiera Robinson is a 2011 graduate of Trotwood-Madison High School. She will continue to pursue writing beyond high school.

Auston Smith is a 2011 graduate of Trotwood-Madison High School. He will attend Ashland University to pursue a career in medicine. He likes to draw, play sports and will continue writing as a way to express himself.

Bobby Smith is a 2011 graduate of Trotwood-Madison High School. He will attend Bowling Green State University to pursue a career in Engineering. He is interested in playing football and writing poetry and rap music.

Davonn Stollings graduates from Trotwood-Madison High School in 2013. He wants to study Medicine at Ohio State University or University of Kentucky. He enjoys skating, basketball and football.

Elisha Street is a 2011 graduate of Trotwood-Madison High School. She plans to study Creative Writing in college to become a writer.

Chrisha Taylor will graduate from Trotwood-Madison High School in 2013. She wants to pursue a career in Cosmetology or Pharmacy. She plans to continue writing.

Jasmine Thompson is a member of Trotwood-Madison's class of 2012. She wants to attend Savanna University, but is still undecided as to what she will study. She loves children and animals. She will continue writing poetry and in her journal.

Tionna Towler will graduate from Trotwood-Madison in 2013. She plans to attend Wright State University or the University of Indiana. Her goal is to be a nurse. She plays soccer and enjoys helping in her community.

Renika Williams is a 2011 graduate of Trotwood-Madison High School. She will be attending Wright State University to pursue Acting and Communications/Broadcasting. She thrives in the performing arts and will continue to write through her love of language and poetry.

Tonisha Williamson is a 2011 graduate of Trotwood-Madison High School. She plans to attend the University of Akron to study Pharmacy. She participates in JROTC.

Asha Wooten is a 2011 graduate of Trotwood-Madison High School. She will attend Kentucky State University to pursue a career in Public Health. She is interested in fashion, music and health. She writes about everything that inspires her.

Passionate Pens

Edited by Valerie L. Coleman

In 2006, Valerie J. Lewis Coleman, took her writing and publishing curriculum to prisons and schools. The following year, the first **Passionate Pens** book—*Tainted Mirror An Anthology*—debuted. The book is a call to action to stop making excuses, walk in purpose and fulfill destiny.

The objective of the program is to promote literacy by

- Exposing students to the book-publishing industry
- Compiling and publishing writings by the students
- Providing each contributor with a copy of the anthology
- Establishing creditability as published authors
- Debuting the anthology at the Dayton Book Expo
- Offering this program FREE to participating students
- Generating revenue for the sponsoring institution

To learn more about how to implement this program at your school, visit

PassionatePens.com

Trotwood-Madison High School Creative Writing 2010-2011

Pen of the Writer

*Out of Ephraim was there a root of them against Amalek; after thee, Benjamin, among thy people; out of Machir came down governors, and out of Zebulun they that handle the **pen of the writer**.*
~ Judges 5:14

Pen Of the WritER

A publishing company committed to using the writing pen as a weapon to fight the enemy and celebrate the good news of Christ Jesus.

Taking writers from pen to paper to published!

Passionate Pens
Write On! Workshop
Pen to Paper Literary Symposium
Literary Coaching & Consultation

Pen of the Writer, LLC
Dayton, Ohio
PenOfTheWriter.com
info@PenOfTheWriter.com

A Kingdom Waiting: Loss, Triumph and the Young Spirit

To order additional copies of

A Kingdom Waiting: Loss, Triumph and the Young Spirit

Trotwood Madison Senior High School
Attention: Sarah Acton
4440 North Union Road
Trotwood, Ohio 45426
937.854.0878

* * * * * * * * * * * * * * * *

Name:	
Address:	
City, State Zip:	
Email:	
Phone:	( )

Quantity	Price Per Book	Total
	$9.95	
Shipping ($2.49 first book, $0.99 each additional)		
Grand Total* (Payable to: Trotwood Madison)		

* Certified check and money orders only

Also Available on Amazon.com

www.ingramcontent.com/pod-product-compliance
Lightning Source LLC
Chambersburg PA
CBHW031300290426
44109CB00012B/651